Babel

Pitt Poetry Series

Ed Ochester, Editor

Babel

Barbara Hamby

University of Pittsburgh Press

The publication of this book is supported by a grant from the
Pennsylvania Council on the Arts

This book is the winner of the 2003 Donald Hall Prize in Poetry, awarded by the
Association of Writers and Writing Programs. AWP, a national organization
serving over 300 colleges and universities, has its headquarters at George Mason
University, Tallwood House, Mail Stop 1E3, Fairfax, Va. 22030.

for Richard Howard

Contents

I

The Mockingbird Blues

And you shall rise up at the voice of the bird,
and all the daughters of musick shall be brought low.

ECCLESIASTES 12: 4

Adieu! The fancy cannot cheat so well
As she is fam'd to do, deceiving elf.

JOHN KEATS
"Ode to a Nightingale"

My Translation

I am translating the world into mockingbird, into blue jay,
 into cat-bombing avian obbligato, because I want
more noise, more bells, more senseless tintinnabulation,
 more crow, thunder, squawk, more bird song,
more Beethoven, more philharmonic mash notes to the gods.
 I am translating the world into onyx, into Abyssinian,
into pale blue Visigoth vernacular, because the bloody earth
 is not one color, one stripe, one smooth mulatto
café con leche cream-colored dream, no rumba, no cha-cha,
 no cheek-to-cheek tango through the Argentinian
midnight stream, but a hodgepodge of rival factions
 fighting over the borders of nothing. I am translating
the world into blue, azure, cerulean, because there is a sky
 beneath us as there is a sea above. O the fish soar
like dragonflies through empyrean clouds; the mockingbird
 swims through the ocean like a man-of-war. I am
translating the heavens into Gutenberg, into Bodoni,
 into offset digital karmic Palatino, every "T" a crucifix
on the shrine of my lexicographic longing. I am reading
 the archaic language of birches, frangipani pidgin of monsoon,
Bali palm dialect of endless summer. I am translating the sky
 into bulls, swans, gold dust, for a god is filled with such power
that mortal husbands quiver in the shadow of his furious lust,
 the bliss-driven engine of his thrumming mythopoesis.
I am calling the world to take off its veils of fog and soot,
 shed its overcoat of factories, highways, skyscrapers,
lay down its rocks, roots, rivers, and lie naked in my naked arms,
 for I am translating the earth and all its dominions
into desire, into flayed skin screaming abandon, all tongue,
 mouth, flesh-drunk erotic demonology, fiery seraphim
mating with mortals, wings incinerated in the white heat

of love, Apollo turning Daphne into marble, into tree roots,
into chlorophyll, scent of cut grass, a baby's mouth sweet
    with milk, because this is my Cultural Revolution,
my Mao Tse Tung, my Chou En-Lai, my attempt to go
    without sin, to have it my way no matter what, for I am
the way, the truth, the light, third empress of the seventh dynasty,
    Madame Chiang, Madame Nhu, Madame X, Madame
Three Quarters of the Left Brain, poster girl of a million GIs,
    Betty Grable to you, buster, Jane Russell, all gams, breasts,
blonde smiles, brunette tribulation, Betty and Veronica,
    the last stop before Kiss-and-Tell, Texas, Fourth
Shepherdess of confabulation, Calliope's stepdaughter, Erato's
    girl, it's all Greek to me, for I am translating the world
as if it were a bomb, a thief, a book. Chapter One: the noun
    of my mother's womb, verb of birth, adjectives of blood,
screams, fluorescence. Chapter Two: explosions of words
    growing into sentences, arms, legs, tentacles. Chapter Three:
voyages to unheard-of territories—here be monsters, two-mile
    waterfalls, portals to the underworld. Chapter Four: returns,
for in all of us there's an Odysseus ready to misunderstand the sky
    and its garbled signs, rumble-thunder theater of missed cues,
because this is our adventure, our calling, our do-or-die
    mission, translating the world into the body's bright lie.

The Mockingbird on the Buddha

The mockingbird on the Buddha says, Where's my seed,
    you Jezebel, where's the sunshine in my blue sky,
where's the Hittite princess, Pharaoh's temple, where's the rain
    for the misery I love so much? The mockingbird
on the Buddha scolds the tree for trying to stay straight
    in the hurricane of words blowing out of the cold north,
wind like screams, night like brandy on the dark cut of my heart.
    The mockingbird on the Buddha, music is his life,
he hears the tunes of the universe, cacophony of calypso,
    hacking cough in the black lung of desire; he's ruddy
with lust, that sweet stepping puffed-up old grey bird o' mine.
    The mockingbird on the Buddha says, Eat up
while the night is young. Have some peach cobbler, girl,
    have some fried oysters, have some Pouligny
Montrachet, *ma chère*, for the night is coming, and you need meat
    on your bones to ride that wild horse. The mockingbird
on the Buddha says, It's time for a change, little missy. You've
    been in charge too long. It's time for the bird
to take over, because he stays up late, knows what night can be,
    past 1 2, past two, when trouble's dark and beautiful.
You never knew what hit you, and that's the best feeling
    in the whole wide world. The mockingbird
on the Buddha makes his nest inside my brain: he looks good
    in grey, gets fat on thought, he's my enemy,
my Einstein, my ever-loving monkey boy, every monkey thought
    I blame on him, every night so sweet my body breaks
apart like a Spanish galleon raining gold on the ocean floor.

The History of Apples, Part One

There's Eve with her apple patter——*You're gonna love*
    this, honey, this is gonna feel so good in the godforsaken

marrow of your narrow hips, so good God said, you better
    not. That good, she said with her apple butter, bitter nut

of her sly squint, quaint paint of her mouth like a pear,
    almost split apart before you take the first sweet bite,

that sweet. You almost think you're drowning, and you are,
    under water so deep, you'll never be on dry land again.

You're swimming, baby, doing the backstroke, butterfly,
    breaststroke right to the edge of the world, and before you

drop off, you think, *What was I thinking?* Only you weren't
    thinking, were you? No sir, thinking's something you do

with your brain, and that's not what you were using, buddy.
    You were on a different train altogether, and it took you

from Oasis Central to this sandstorm of knuckle busting,
    rock breaking, plowing and planting. Call it agriculture

if you want: I call it slaving, no more lazing about all day,
    naming the animals——rhinoceros, kangaroo, dingo,

mockingbird. You're in the factory now, 24 hours a day,
    seven days a week, no more sweet nothing, no more sweet

apple calling, *Come here, darling, come to Mama,* with a voice
    like corn syrup, breasts like honeydews. Oh, honey, don't

do me like that, supper's over and I'm tired of wanting, tired
    of waiting for another drink from my mama's sweet mouth.

Idolatry

My Baal, shimmering Apollo, junkyard Buonarroti,
    funkadelic *malocchio*, voice shouting
from the radio, talking about love, about heartbreak,
    about doing everything you can till you cain't do
no more. Then you float by in a Coupe de Ville,
    hair conked, wearing the mink stole
of delicious indifference, reciting the odes
    of Mr. John Keats like you wuz his best friend.
I was minding my own business, being good as a girl
    can be when every inch of skin aches
for the sky. Where is my wide sky, now all I see
    is you? Where is my ocean, you hex on thought,
golden calf in the living room of ambition, pagan call,
    demon whispering like beetles on the skin
of morning. I hear your voice come out of the mouths
    of little girls jumping rope on Orange Avenue.
I hear your aria in the shopping center pharmacy,
    in the tired lines around the eyes
of every sleepless night. You're an astronomer,
    roaming the heavens, a flyboy anatomist,
dissecting the stars. Tell me again about the stars,
    those cheap flashcards of the gods. Tell me
about human sacrifice, the huju rituals of versification,
    the quantum mechanics of line, my holy-of-holies,
sanctum sanctorum, my hideaway in the world of cool.
    Pagan huckster, heat up your spells, your charms,
your rapture, I come to you a novice, an acolyte,
    a scullery maid in the choir of the unruly. Give me
my music, my words, my lyrical demonstration
    of all that is gorgeous and invisible. I am
your handmaiden, your courtesan, your ten-cents-a-dance

barroom floozie. My Lord-who-whispers-his-secrets-
into-the-skulls-of-angels, your slightest whim is my delight.
 Every day I wake to your disciples' quick trill.
I am the prisoner of your darkest sigh, queen of ungovernable
 birds. You visit me at night when the sky is a veil
of stars, your shame an aphrodisiac, a love potion,
 a quick fix in the alley from the dark drug of words.

O Deceitful Tongue

You love all words that devour, O deceitful tongue.

PSALMS 52:4

Rogue slab in the slaughterhouse of the mouth,
you love all words that whistle like bombs

through the delphinium sky. O tongue that sucks
honey from the vinegar bush—demagogue, street

preacher, cutpurse at the afternoon hanging—break
my neck a thousand times till I remember the digits

of your prime number. Drunk tongue, warling,
malt-mad forger in the bone orchard, give me

your traitor's code, so I can whistle my psalm
through the sinworm night. Tongue of rough

bread, blues tongue, wolf tongue. Kiss me,
deceitful mouth, smash my curtain of skin, devour

the air wild with bees, swallow their wings,
make me a bloody hive for their bitter queen.

The Mockingbird Counts to Ten

A bird is a diabolic creation, half animal, half angel, rodent
    heart, cherubim wings, blood red as the Roman sky
at sunset, Barberini bees circling the fort. One
    can never tell how life will end, perhaps in the street
outside your hotel, run down by a fat, drunken man
    in a Mercedes, a friend holding you in her arms,
wailing like a bird, an eagle diving for his prey. Oh, pray now,
    my pretty, as the light fades, *carabinieri* filling out forms,
witnesses railing at the drunk, your legs like two broken vases
    gone golden in the summer light. *Oh, the three men
I admire the most, the father, son, holy ghost*, squeaks the radio,
    Madonna of the air waves in the Holy City
and in the sky ten thousand black birds. Pray now,
    before they shut your eyes forever. Oh, a bird
can tell you anything you want to know, Kristallnacht
    on every corner, gestapo heart beating in every chest,
come five o'clock like clockwork, the work day ends
    and the cocktail hour begins, martini, margarita,
Manhattan. The more you drink the less you forget: six
    million Jews, two million Catholics, anarchists, gypsies,
Bosnians, Hutus, Tutsis, intellectuals, Commies, punks,
    murderers. Oh, misfits of the world, unite
or when you reign remember the thrill of blood in your veins,
    paper-thin, the wall of skin, between liquid you
and the queasy world like Michelangelo Merisi's teeming
    Seven Acts of Mercy locked in a church in Naples,
I will never see because it is *in restauro* forever. The mockingbird
    ate the lark and the nightingale, because there's no
rest for the wicked. *No*, says the dying woman. *Nein*,
    says the quivering fraulein *Unter den linden*. Evil is as evil
does, says someone very close to you, Vlad the Impaler

or one of your other best friends. You certainly know
how to pick 'em, know who will murder you for a nickel,
        so to ward off the undead you draw a big X on the path,
because the duppy can't count to ten. Yowling with rage,
        he has to start over at one, and there's nothing
more irritable than a zero with no other number to give it
        a shoulder up into the world of dollars and scents.

The Mockingbird Falls in Love

Call her Mama, Baby, Darling, but she's nobody's girl,
leading lady of the cathouse delirium, librarian of all

you'll never know, *la belle dame sans merci*. She calls the shots,
has the hots for every leather-jacket-wearing Sal Mineo

wanna-be who ever sculpted a perfect curl over his third eye,
resolved to quit smashing the nose of his one and only, died

in a fiery crash. She's scrubwoman in the workhouse of love.
She pays the piper, predicts the future, spreads her cards,

always comes up with the Devil or Death. She's the twitch
in your gut, oil fire in your stomach, flutter in your heart,

the high-five beehive of righteousness, your highness,
jive princess of the pornographic opera, CAT scan

of your deepest desires. You look at the marks of her
perfect teeth on your heart and say, Bite me, bite me again.

Run

You want to get out of town like a two-bit hood on the hoof
    from the law, smuggling marijuana in some inner crevice
of a baby-blue Impala, not like a patch of bad luck, not walking,
    but picking up your feet like Jim Ryun breaking
the four-minute mile or, better yet, a 1944 Desoto racing a Model T.
    You don't have a car, but Greyhound goes everywhere,
local or express, creeping like kudzu up a telephone pole.
    Oh yeah, you're that girl on the bus, skipping town
like a jackrabbit or the second hand on a watch, because time's
    on the move and all you have is debts. That man
handed you a bill no girl could pay. The story was a front page
    headline: *If He's Working So Much Overtime,*
Why Isn't He Bringing Home More Money? You suspected
    something, the sunny thought flitting across the television
screen of your mind like a bee going from dandelion to daisy,
    but who wants to pull the rug from under her own life,
even if it's full of holes, ratty as a cheap toupee? Rumors flew
    all over town but never stung you. You were sailing
before the wind until seated one fine October day at the piano,
    fingers wandering over the keys, you picked out a melody
like kids wild in the streets, like a letter you didn't even have to read,
    your eyes passing over the words the way you breathe
in a bad dream, quick and hard, so hard it hurts, but nothing
    comes from your mouth, no words, no scream,
you just wait until darkness grabs you like a monster. Or maybe
    you try to get past that particular Cyclops,
but your life's still like a bar tab that's gotten away from you
    or a bath that's spilling over, and you're not even drunk
but you're probably drowning, hanging with the weirdest people.
    You don't even like them and they hate you, stab
you in the back when you leave the room. Your shirt's so bloody,

you'll never get out the stains, and you've even thought
of eloping with your ex-husband, who squandered your inheritance
of beauty and good will. No, that subscription's finished,
the magazine filled with stories more boring than your own.
Why even that old mockingbird makes fun of you,
squawkin' through the ragged afternoon, though in the long
tedious trajectory of your life nothing matters
because time will stop someday like an old bus sputtering
into a busted town in Nevada or New Mexico,
spark plugs corroded, springs poking through the seats,
and you'll get off the bus, brush the dust
from your threadbare skirt, look up at a big grey sky as empty
as time itself, and for once you'll feel a glimmer
of something sweet in your heart, like that smell of turned earth
in April when you were little, the raw cold of winter gone,
but July still a dream, and you'll think, so this is happiness,
because there'll be nowhere left to run.

Vex Me

Vex me, O Night, your stars stuttering like a stuck jukebox,
put a spell on me, my bones atremble at your tabernacle

of rhythm and blues. Call out your archers, chain me
to a wall, let the stone fortress of my body fall

like a rabid fox before an army of dogs. Rebuke me,
rip out my larynx like a lazy snake and feed it to the voiceless

throng. For I am midnight's girl, scouring unlit streets
like Persephone stalking her swarthy lord. Anoint me

with oil, make me greasy as a fast-food fry. Deliver me
like a pizza to the snapping crack-house hours between

one and four. Build me an ark, fill it with prairie moths,
split-winged fritillaries, blue-bottle flies. Stitch

me a gown of taffeta and quinine, starlight and nightsoil,
and when the clock tocks two, I'll be the belle of the malaria ball.

As always the world was a mess, nobody understanding
    a thing, two weeks after
Babel when God pulled the rug out from under creation,
    messed it up good. What in heaven's name
could I do, just sit there with everyone jabbering
    like monkeys? So I got busy, couldn't sit on my
duff forever contemplating the infinite. Anyway, the world
    was smaller then,
everything between the Tigris and Euphrates. *Mesopotamia*,
    now there's a fabulous word. I
found it under a rock at a bazaar in Babylon. At first
    it was simple—counting amphoras of oil, cattle,
goats—but humans know a good thing when they see it.
    Pretty soon they were making up
horror stories. *Gilgamesh*, my God, those Assyrians
    were inventive people, but the Egyptians—
Isis, Ra, Set, Thoth, the jackal-headed god. For 2,500
    years, not until the King
James Bible did I hear a translation of God's word that sent
    such a shiver up my spine, rocked my
kundalini to the stars. Chinese, a gorgeous lingo,
    but all those perfect
little pictures: I tried to talk them out of it. Limits
    their poetry in
my not-so-humble opinion, but they had their own ideas.
    Everyone does, don't they?
Now Arabic, there's a poetic language, good-looking, too,
    like a river running through the fingers.
Oh, God wasn't all that fond of writing at first, a little
    jealous if you ask me,
pouted for a couple thousand years. Woke up with

the Children of Israel up to their necks in
quicksand, stranded in the desert, as ragged-looking
    a group as you'd ever hope to see, Moses
raging at God, writing it all down. Nothing like a good
    book to soothe a savage deity, and Moses
saying God was in charge. He liked that. Yes sir,
    something not a little bit
Teutonic about Jehovah, though Deutschland came later.
    Charming language German: *Schadenfreude,*
Übermensch, Scheissbedauren, regret that something's
    not as bad as you'd hoped it would be. Take
Vienna, 1900, almost religious in its incapacitation,
    how desperately it needed Freud. Wien, not unlike
wein, wine, whine. Oh, words, my darling liebchens,
    how I adore you—in cuneiform, pictographs,
xenophobic Fascist diatribes, the *Mahabharata,* Lao-Tzu,
    Krazy Kat's smacks and pows, *Das Kapital,*
yellow journalism, Yorick's skull, yabba-dabba-do.
    From Katmandu to the zebra-striped farms of
Zimbabwe, the world is singing my tune, backyard chat,
    blue-streak phat, the mockingbird's yakety-yak.

Fang

I want to be seven feet tall, walk out of the Gabon bush,
    speaking Fang, to gaze into the sky and see
        an overturned bowl of godless blue, a wild storm
in the heart of the devil, a rocky sea of scudding,
        poisoned boats. I want to look into the dark canopy
of trees and hear the mother of all talking creatures,
fluttering mountains, a green sea swimming with fish that fly.
    I need Fang for revenge—fire smoldering
        in the heart, a quick knife, a sickness
that fells grown men in the midday sun. I want words
    like teeth that could tear the flesh
        from the throat of my worst enemy—her face
    staring at me from every mirror. Every morning
my voice is a bird flying over treetops,
        dropping berries bitter and sweet
    into mouths open and closed. I can hardly bear
the sun on my skin. O Fang, come to me as a suitor
    with two goats and an orchard of pomegranates, woo me
        with your straight back, take me deep
into the night when stars fall like faithless lovers
    on the black trees. I need the mouth of a viper,
        a vampire, a mad dog pulling children
    from their mothers' arms. I want my heart to swell
like a wide brown river carrying trees, huts, limbs
        to the flood-maddened sea. O Fang,
    heart of a snake, body of impenetrable water,
        dark continent of betel nut and monkeypod,
erupt from my tongue, give me a world I cannot give myself.

Thus Spake the Mockingbird

The mockingbird says, hallelujah, coreopsis, I make the day
    bright, I wake the night-blooming jasmine. I am
the duodecimo of desperate love, the hocus-pocus passion
    flower of delirious retribution. You never saw such a bird,
such a triage of blood and feathers, tongue and bone. O the world
    is a sad address, bitterness melting the tongues of babies,
breasts full of accidental milk, but I can teach the flowers to grow,
    take their tight buds, unfurl them like flags in the morning heat,
fat banners of scent, flat platters of riot on the emerald scene.
    I am the green god of pine trees, conducting the music
of rustling needles through a harp of wind. I am the heart of men,
    the wild bird that drives their sex, forges their engines,
jimmies their shattered locks in the dark flare where midnight slinks.
    I am the careless minx in the skirts of women, the bright moon
caressing their hair, the sharp words pouring from their beautiful mouths
    in board rooms, on bar stools, in big city laundrettes. I am
Lester Young's sidewinding sax, sending that Pony Express
    message out west in the Marconi tube hidden in every torso
tied tight in the corset of do and don't, high and low, yes and no. I am
    the radio, first god of the twentieth century, broadcasting
the news, the blues, the death counts, the mothers wailing
    when everyone's gone home. I am sweeping
through the Eustachian tubes of the great plains, transmitting
    through every ear of corn, shimmying down the spine
of every Bible-thumping banker and bureaucrat, relaying the anointed
    word of the shimmering world. Every dirty foot that walks
the broken streets moves on my wings. I speak from the golden
    screens. Hear the roar of my discord murdering the trees,
screaming its furious rag, the fuselage of my revival-tent brag. Open
    your windows, slip on your castanets. I am the flamenco
in the heel of desire. I am the dancer. I am the choir. Hear my wild
    throat crowd the exploding sky. O I can make a noise.

II

13 Ways of Looking at Paris

I was of three minds
Like a tree
In which there are three blackbirds.
                    WALLACE STEVENS

Babel

Assyrian for gate of God, behold our present bedlam,
    ziggurat of steel, zeitgeist of bread and 2000 cheeses,
behold its gothic towers, the stutter of its engines,
    yammering madmen, black-jacketed girls
colliding with the morning on the Pont Marie, children passing
    x-rated marquees at the Place Pigalle. Behold the
dark lord of the metro, his maze of tracks, his trains
    winding through the underworld, clacking
elephants on tightropes of metal and fire. Give me a glass of
    vin rouge, give me the machine gun of the sidewalk
flic, give me a slide down the Champs-Elysées with Père
    Ubu the Übermensch of the down-and-out, Aloha
Götterdämmerung, twilight of the dogs. Behold my tangled
    thoughts like prisoners on a windowless train to Poland,
hullabaloo of the knacker house—if I'm so goddamned
    smart, why do I keep cutting off my fingers? The id-
id-idiot princess who shares my skull, her skills
    resemble nothing more than the damson plum jam
jars that lined 19th-century pantries. Behold my brother's
    404, a Peugeot on Quaaludes, and the ratty
klebs bark "Bow wow, ooh la la." While this century's
    party is winding down, we're cranking up the gears,
lubricating the sexual apparatus of the next thousand years.
    O baby, baby, sweet baby, sometimes I am nothing
more than a mouth, eating more than my share, saying
    nothing with more ruffles than an Elizabethan
nobleman—*Aphrodite tongues, lumbago delirium, fritillarious*
    malcontent. You speak French with an odd accent,
Ohio via Puhano Street, and it comes out sounding
    like a hillbilly with a mouth full of grits. O
Parigi, Pa-ree, Paris, Texas, to you Wim Wenders, eine

kleine Dippity-doo. Tristan Tzara takes off his tiara and says,
Qu'est-ce que c'est? I'd be the last one to know because
    Je suis a hundred thousand voices in one
redolent sack of flesh, whizzing like a Flash Gordon space slave
    in the rush-hour metro between Mabillon and
Sèvres-Babylone where the ghost station hides my
    hideous thoughts like circus freaks—bearded, wild-eyed, ten
toes on every foot, this little piggy never goes home, never
    goes home, too many rivers to cross, too many
underground caverns to light with the nonexistent
    flame of my spiritual radiance. An amateur
ventriloquist in the house of the deaf, I throw my voice,
    enter the magic theater, climb the magic mountain, fly into the
wild blue yonder, for I'm on an escapade, a cross-dressing
    dyslexic roller-coaster ride through the high-minded,
x-ray funhouse of my own rattle-trap time on earth,
    certain there is a message just for me. Be it yodel,
yip, or yes siree, it's mysterious as the tuba of the metro
    busker deep in the rumble of his own blues,
Zola's *J'accuse* echoing in the branches along the Île St.-Louis,
    all the brave new words, abracadabra, *le dernier cri*.

Cinerama

When moviegoers die, instead of paradise they go to Paris,
    for where else can you find 300 screens
showing nearly every film you'd want to see, not to mention movies
    like *Captain Blood*, in which bad boy Errol Flynn
buckles his swash across the seven seas, and though I'm not dead,
    I may be in heaven, walking down the rue St.-Antoine,
making lists of my favorite movies, number one being Cocteau's
    Beauty and the Beast, but I'm with Garbo at the end:
"Where is my beast? Give me my beast." Oh, the beasts have it
    on the silver screen——*Ivan the Terrible*, *M*, *Nosferatu*,
The Mummy——all misshapen, murderous monsters,
    because no matter how beautiful we are, inside we know
ourselves to be bloodsucking vampires, zombies, freaks cobbled
    together with spare parts from the graveyard,
and God some kind of Dr. Frankenstein or megalomaniacal director,
    part nice-guy Frank Capra, yes, but the other part
Otto Preminger, bald, with Nazi tics, because the world
    is beautiful and hideous at the same time,
an identical Technicolor sky over us all, and the stars. Who came up
    with that concept——the distance, the light,
the paparazzi flash? And the dialogue, which is sometimes snappy
    or *très poétique*, as if written by Shakespeare himself,
then at other times by the most guttural Neanderthal on the planet,
    grubbing his way across the landscape, noticing the sky
only when it becomes his enemy or friend, dark with birds,
    not Hitchcock's, but dinner, throwing rocks into the sky,
most of them missing their target, a few bouncing off his prognathous jaw,
    like Kubrick with his cavemen and spacemen existing
on the same continuum, a Möbius strip to be sure but with Strauss,
    both Richard and Johann, in the background, and though it's winter
there's a waltz in the air as I walk through the Place des Vosges,

and I'm still trying to come up with number two,
maybe *400 Blows* or *Breathless*, because here I am, after all, in Paris
still expecting to see Belmondo and Seberg racing
down the street, cops after them, bullets flying, and maybe I am
in heaven, but I'll always be waiting for Godard.

Ode to the Potato

"They eat a lot of French fries here," my mother
        announces after a week in Paris, and she's right,
not only about *les pommes frites* but the celestial tuber
        in all its forms: *rotie, purée*, not to mention
au gratin or boiled and oiled in *la salade niçoise*.
        Batata edulis discovered by gold-mad conquistadors
in the West Indies, and only a 100 years later
        in *The Merry Wives of Windsor* Falstaff cries,
"Let the skie raine Potatoes," for what would we be
        without you—lost in a sea of fried turnips,
mashed beets, roasted parsnips? *Mi corazón, mon coeur,*
        my core is not the heart but the stomach, tuber
of the body, its hollow stem the throat and esophagus,
        leafing out to the nose and eyes and mouth. Hail
the conquering spud, all its names marvelous: *Solanum*
        tuberosum, *Igname*, Caribe, Russian Banana, Yukon Gold.
When you turned black, Ireland mourned. O Mr. Potato Head,
        how many deals can a man make before he stops being
small potatoes? How many men can a woman drop
        like a hot potato? Eat it cooked or raw like an apple
with salt of the earth, apple of the earth, *pomme de terre*.
        Tuber, tuber burning bright in a kingdom without light,
deep within the earth where the Incan potato gods rule,
        forging their golden orbs for the world's ravening gorge.

Left Bank Freudian Striptease

The only problem with seeing Racine's *Phèdre* three
times in as many weeks is they're all jumbled inside me

like Freud's triad mating with *The Three Faces of Eve*.
In London the ego—Eve White is the tragic queen,

while in Paris, the id at the Odéon, Eve B.,
rips off her skimpy gown, so the audience can feast

its eyes on her pert breasts, taut abdomen, coppery
delta, and though I'm crazy about redheads, for me

it's the one-man show on the tiny stage in the 14th
I find myself returning to——a superannuated superego

for our times. Oh, he can do you the lust, the tragedy,
youthful longing, the handmaiden's evil goading, fleeing

prince. Like a god, he's a zeppelin above the sorties
of the other two: ego tied to earth, id's striptease

in Hell, strutting, all secrets blabbed, twirling pasties
sparkling under lights. And when is lust not like burning

in the Underworld, sulfurous but, at the same time, silly:
the ridiculous suicide attempts, tight skirts, spike heels

of desire, or the housewife of yearning, hardly a queen,
feet on terra firma or incognita as the case may be,

washing the dishes of her predicament. Give me
the Eve called Jane, bald man on a bare stage, all poetry,

no person, all passion in the language, the soaring
couplets, so unlike the characters in the play: the king,

his wife, his son, and the playgoer, in the dark, alone,
watching them all, as if it were no one's life but her own.

Calling the Friends of Friends

for Phyllis Moore

When I call my best friend to tell her I'll be living
        in Paris, she says I have to telephone her cousin,
the product of one of those marriages concocted
        at the end of World War II,
which might have seemed like a good idea
        when everyone was rollicking through Paris,
the Nazis shellacked and their Krauten sausage cuisine,
        to boot, but less than ideal back in Kansas
and Iowa, too Protestant for their own good, no *couture*
        to speak of much less wine or edible bread,
so this man's mother hotfooted it back to Paris
        so fast he was born in the City of Light,
but with an American last name and a passel of cousins,

one of whom is my friend, possibly the best friend
        in the history of the world, so I promise
I'll telephone him, not because I want to but because she
        wants me to, and I've met the cousin,
who is a lot of fun and handsome, but when I call
        I get his French wife who is bitter
with a capital B because her husband is American
        in name only and has some Gallic predilections
a wife rarely finds amusing, and though this bitter
        French wife likes my friend, she does not know
or have any use for me, which is probably a credit
        to her inestimable good sense,
and when I put down the phone, I swear I will never make

such a call again but a few weeks later when another friend
        says she met the grandson of a famous
French movie star, and he really likes American poets,

30

a group of which I am a member, so why
don't I give him a call, and against my better judgment,
    I do, and it's the same scenario, though he makes
the bitter wife of my friend's cousin seem like chairwoman
    of the neighborhood welcoming committee, in fact
he is so unenthusiastic about meeting me I begin to feel sorry
    for him and try to help him out of his unfortunate
predicament, saying, *Oh, never mind, I think I'm coming down*
    with a cold or *I'll call back when we're both less*
busy or *Perhaps the world will end*, and by the time

I'm finished he's dying to see me, but I don't want
    to meet him or anyone else because I'm finished
as a social being, and like the bitter French wife
    I'm unamused, because the only people
who end up entertaining me usually turn out to be mentally ill
    at the very least, but laughter's a drug,
and I'll do almost anything for a laugh, even put up with people
    who hate me until I finally give up, banish them.
And what happens? They all want to be my friend again,
    like the woman with whom I shared an office.
One day she blew up and screamed, *Everyone thinks*
    you're so great, but I see through you.
And she probably did, but who cares? I, for one, did not,

because I am fully conversant with my hideous qualities
    and have striven all my days, like St. Francis feeding
the birds, to render them charming, a not inconsiderable
    task, and years later I would run into this woman
at a bagel shop, and she'd try to touch me and say my name
    in a really warm way, and finally I had to remind her,
We're not friends. Jesus, what is it with people? Like this guy
    who's the adulterous boyfriend of a former friend,
who took me aside and said, *You and Medea*
    should really patch it up. Why? It was 20 years ago,

and someone who has betrayed you once
      is not particularly good friend material in my opinion.
It would be like going back to a car dealer and saying,

I love my Pinto. Can I have another one, please? So I'm vowing
      not to make any new friends and not to use
the telephone or even answer it, because, as Dorothy Parker
      said when her telephone rang, *What fresh hell this?*
Precisely, my darling. How many great phone calls
      have you gotten in your life? I can think
of seven or eight max, and then there are the 100 million
      others staining the hours like the blood
on Lady Macbeth's hands. And the most fabulous thing
      about living in Paris is no one calls,
and it seems a miracle, because there is only one call
      we are ever really expecting, the one at three
in the morning telling you your mother, brother, best friend,

or beloved is dead or maybe even yourself because in many ways
      you've been dead for years though you're
still eating oysters every chance you get, stuffing down
      the *moelleux au chocolat* at Dalloyau, smiling
like a debutante on amphetamines though your heart feels
      like the dessert on the plate in front of you,
broken by a diabolical fork and oozing a thick liquid
      that could be blood though it's probably chocolate
but bitter and hot, words like crumbs in your throat,
      while your fellow diners are answering cell phones,
chatting merrily or dialing as if death and madness
      weren't stalking them as avidly as they're hunting you
down the boulevards and avenues like a diabolic game

of spin-the-bottle. Oh, Death has your number, it's in a book,
      maybe black, maybe not, but he's there waiting
for the right moment, following you down the dark diagonal

of the rue de l'Odéon, sitting near you in your favorite café
on the Place d'Italie, thumbing through mysteries
in the next aisle at the American Library,
standing across the street as you ogle shoes designed
as if in a chthonic collaboration between Mother Teresa
and the Marquis de Sade, dancing with the samurai
roller-bladers as they dodge cars
on the Pont Marie, blowing newspapers and rags
off the homeless man asleep on the rue St.-Antoine,
so ask not for whom the telephone rings. It rings for thee.

Six, Sex, Say

Do you think they wanted sex? asks the naive girl
  in the film about a *femme fatale* who betrays
just about everyone stupid enough to get involved
  with her, but since they are in New Zealand
it sounds like, *Do you think they wanted six?*
  which is another question altogether,
and I know if I were doing drugs I would think
  this was possibly a key to unraveling
the mysteries of the universe, because six in French
  is *cease*, which could mean stop
to one of another linguistic persuasion,
  as in cease and desist, though it could mean six
and desist, and you don't have to study the Kabbala
  to know numbers are powerful, or how to explain
a system invented by Phoenician traders to keep track
  of inventory being used by Einstein,
Dirac, Bohr to describe the mechanics of the universe,
  and even the Marquis de Sade in his long exile
in the Bastille and other dungeons invented
  a numerical code to hide his hideous imagination
from the thought police in that particular patch
  of hell. *Six*, he might cry, but what would he mean,
especially if addressing his pregnant Italian
  mistress, because six is *s-e-i* in Italian,
pronounced *say*. *Say what?* you might say. *Girlfriend,*
  you don't need drugs, and you're absolutely right,
a conclusion I myself came to rather quickly,
  because I'm crossing the Alps now like Psyche
on Cupid's wings, and in German it's *s-e-c-h-s* or sex again,
  in other words, sex of one, half a dozen of another,
which for not-so-unfathomable reasons recalls

Rembrandt's etching of his friend Jan Six
who later became mayor of Amsterdam, a bustling port
    in those days, and visited by one of the last ships
to leave Japan before it closed itself to the outside
    world, and Rembrandt buying the final shipment
of Japanese paper in the west for 200 years. I see
    him in his studio, counting each lovely sheet,
Jan Six in the next room smoking a pipe,
    and I don't know what six is in Dutch,
but it's taking its place in the circle of sixes
    girdling the globe, the Satanic triple six,
the two sixes in my college telephone number, the hidden
    sixes in every deck of cards. *Two plus four,*
three plus three, chant the six-year-olds of the world,
    all their sixes adding up to something, or why
would the psychic have told my friend
    he would never have any money until his address
added up to six, because six is the money number,
    the mysterious key to regeneration,
if not the alpha then the omega, and I who am living
    at 15 quai de Bourbon know that one and five are six,
cease, sex, say, I'm in the money, if the money
    is Paris, and I'm a fool walking her golden streets.

Flesh, Bone, and Red

Looking at Rubens's panels for Marie de Medicis
    in the Louvre with Stuart, whom my husband
calls Maria Stuarda for no other reason
    than the Italian rolls off his tongue
so sweetly and I think of how he wooed me
    with a barrage of words so cunningly fluent,
so linguistically adroit, I was caught like a dragonfly
    in a spider's web, a delicious death,
but here we are older and not particularly wiser
    in Paris, and Stuart is walking with one boot off
because of arthritis in her foot, and my big toe
    aches intermittently from a dance injury,
and I carry the x-ray with me, if for nothing else
    to contemplate the beauty of my bones,
all twenty six, delicately rigged,
    somehow more elegant than the foot itself,
and Stuart is explaining Rubens's genius,
    how his choice to separate the two cheeks
of a demi-goddess's buttocks with brick red instead of black
    is glorious, and this room in the former palace
looks like nothing so much as an opera set,
    home of the Scottish princess, red-haired beauty
of Brodsky's poems, but now ensconced in Verdi's opera,
    beheaded by her rival for the English throne,
and sometimes my toe hurts so much I want to cut it off,
    the little I know about blood saving me,
and wine seems to dull the pain so we limp
    through the bitter night to a little restaurant
in the Marais, order a feast, and toast ourselves
    again and again with glasses of rough Corsican red,
though Stuart and I can't stop talking about the flesh

of Rubens's women, its rosiness, its amplitude,
our own bodies growing thicker, more regal with age,
        the glory of youth passing like a runaway train
as we sit in a field of poppies, meal spread
        on blankets, bottles of champagne, paté,
long bayonets of bread, grapes like mermaids' tears,
        with each morsel making our bodies as Rubens
painted his queens, blue by flesh by stroke by red.

Shh

Every opera, symphony, oratorio, contrabass recital
    has its self-appointed gestapos of silence
to quiet the bumptious hillbillies who talk, cough,
    unwrap throat lozenges in the middle
of violin solos, don't know when to clap, and Paris
    is no different, maybe a little worse,
though at the cinema everyone is still reverent,
    knowing that Angelopoulos, Scorsese,
even Benigni deserve our full attention, could tell us
    something deep and gorgeous about life
or even ourselves, or grim and hallucinatory,
    though laughter is okay, I find,
in the squatting-walk sequence of *Il mostro*,
    when the lovers waddle off together,
and I am almost choking in hysterical rapture,
    and no one cares, nor do I, so noise
isn't the problem but the nature of the noise,
    because I'm the most intolerant person I know,
and I know myself pretty well, the fascist inside
    ready to sharpen the guillotine for all the hacking,
sniveling, rustling malefactors, unless it is I
    who am coughing and too in love with Mozart
to stay home, drink tea, and sacrifice my own pleasure
    for that of others, so really I don't know
myself at all or I would recognize the nearsighted
    little girl sitting next to me, my ten-year-old self
with her ugly nylon hairband and nailbitten fingers
    who is clapping after the second movement
of Schubert's "Trio in E minor" because it's the most
    beautiful thing she's ever heard
and moreover a door opening on a life she can only dimly

imagine of poetry, champagne, Paris,
delirious amour, a door behind which a brilliant light
is shining, and even the rancorous tuning
of the orchestra sounds lovely, squawk of violin,
heart-stopping rumble of timpani, low moan of cellos,
and the chandeliers are dimming in the Palais Garnier,
gold-leaf handmaidens of the gods fading,
Chagall's lovers disappearing, so *Shh*, here comes
the conductor, we're in for something divine.

As we sit down for yet another sublime meal
    at Quan Hue on the Avenue de Choisy,
instead of the usual Vietnamese hit parade, a tape
    of Beatles tunes erupts in the quiet room,
not covers, but the Fab Four themselves belting out
    their watered-down rockabilly hits,
beginning with "Ticket to Ride," and all the ultra-chic
    French in the restaurant start swaying back
and forth as if hypnotized by some pop-culture Svengali,
    singing in ridiculous English, "She's gotta teeket
to ri-i-ide," even the sad-looking woman
    and her bored husband wailing like the Hamburg
John Lennon, and when I order my *rouleau de printemps*,
    the waiter is singing, "She woze a daytrippair,
one-way teeket, yeah," and I figure he was about minus
    15 years old when that came out, and his parents,
if they'd even met each other, much less thought of him,
    were dodging bombs my ex-schoolmates
were dropping on their homeland, and when he delivers
    my beer the whole restaurant is singing "Roll Over
Beethoven," conjuring the shadow of those teenaged
    toughs in Liverpool listening to scratchy LPs
of old Delta bluesmen, their pomaded scions,
    the anarchy of Little Richard, luminous misery
of B. B. King, Robert Johnson's tawny grief, down
    as any human being could be, and as I eat my bowl
of *vermicelles avec porc grillé au citronelle*, the tape
    loops back to John Lennon wailing, haranguing
the dark slave of love in the heart of everyone, naked,
    chained by impulses we can hardly control,
trying to understand why our hearts are breaking like a ship

off the stony coast of some unknown new world,
a thunderous storm breaking the masts, the crew washed
        overboard, the captain impaled on the rigging,
misery and greed swept into the vast maw of the hungry ocean,
        and we're in the churning water, unchained at last,
falling down waves steep as mountains, drinking salt
        water as if it were wine, the sun breaking through
purple clouds, and if only we could swim, we might be free.

"In a past life I was all the people in these paintings,"
     my brother says, waving his arms around a gallery
at the Louvre, which includes David's *Coronation*
     of Napoleon and Ingres' naked odalisque,
which I point to and say, "Even her?" "Especially her,"
     he crows, and my 1 2-year-old nephew says,
"Gee, Dad, you sure were sexy." This is the way it goes
     with my family—no one skips a beat till he falls
flat on his face, not that the hula skirt of self-delusion
     hasn't wrapped itself around my mother, sisters,
and me but I'm thinking of the Marquis de Sade
     these days because the big joke in Paris is that tourists
go to the Place Bastille and expect to see a fortress
     and instead find a column with a gilded figure
at the top and twenty concentric circles of demented cars
     whizzing around it like mechanical dogs
after their tails, the Revolution having razed the prison
     as it stripped so many buildings, especially ecclesiastical,
but the bigger joke is that the revolutionary rabble
     were tearing down a prison holding only a few jailbirds,
one of them the corpulent marquis, who loathed the hoi-polloi
     with all his heart if that's what you'd call the organ
pumping in his chest; however, no one could call him a dummy,
     and after the aristocracy was kaput he reinvented
himself as Citizen Sade, time and avoirdupois having taken
     the top off his libido, drama now his passion,
though his plays were so unsavory and he such a pain in the ass,
     no one would stage them, so he published
his prison writings which put him right back in the clink,
     where at least he could produce his plays.
In or out—who's not in a cell of some kind? I'm standing

on the Champs-Elysées on Bastille Day, a kind
of show-off for the French military, and my husband gets all hot
        and bothered when the French girls in uniforms
parade by with machine guns slung over their shoulders.
        There's probably a magazine for him, *Girls with Guns*,
like *Chicks with Dicks*, which I thought was a joke when I first
        heard of it but guess what, we're all living
in the Marquis's world, every corner kiosk stacked with nudie
        magazines and posters of nearly naked models
who look so cold in January, their arms and chests exposed
        to the Arctic winds that bite my face as I pass
a plaque that commemorates the spot where members
        of the Resistance were shot by Nazi occupiers,
and we're all trudging through the winter afternoon,
        my brother, my husband, the French soldiers
in their mini-skirts and machine guns, Danton, his statue
        at the Odéon metro stop dusted with snow,
and the ghosts of Robespierre, Voltaire, and Citizen Sade,
        his overcoat pulled close across his paunch, head circled
by buzzing locusts, wasps, beetles, winged maggots, hornets
        like electrons circling a neutron, a bomb
ready to explode around the next corner, the next century
        when in the giddy years after a war too terrible
to imagine we are free to imagine anything at all.

Ode to American English

I was missing English one day, American, really,
    with its pill-popping Hungarian goulash of everything
from Anglo-Saxon to Zulu, because British English
    is not the same, if the paperback dictionary
I bought at Brentano's on the Avenue de l'Opéra
    is any indication, too cultured by half. Oh, the English
know their dahlias, but what about doowop, donuts,
    Dick Tracy, Tricky Dick? With their elegant Oxfordian
accents, how could they understand my yearning for the hotrod,
    hotdog, hot flash vocabulary of the U. S. of A.,
the fragmented fandango of Dagwood's everyday flattening
    of Mr. Beasley on the sidewalk, fetuses floating
on billboards, drive-by monster hip-hop stereos shaking
    the windows of my dining room like a 7.5 earthquake,
Ebonics, Spanglish, "you know" used as comma and period,
    the inability of 90% of the population to get the past perfect:
I have went, I have saw, I have tooken Jesus into my heart,
    the battle cry of the Bible Belt, but no one uses
the King James anymore, only plain-speak versions,
    in which Jesus, raising Lazarus from the dead, says,
"Dude, wake up," and the L-man bolts up like a B-movie
    mummy. "Whoa, I was toasted." Yes, ma'am,
I miss the mongrel plenitude of American English, its fall-guy,
    rat-terrier, dog-pound neologisms, the bomb of it all,
the rushing River Jordan backwoods mutability of it, the low-rider,
    boom-box cruise of it, from New Joisey to Ha-wah-ya
with its sly dog, malasada-scarfing beach blanket lingo
    to the ubiquitous Valley Girl's *like-like* stuttering,
shopaholic rant. I miss its quotidian beauty, its querulous
    back-biting righteous indignation, its preening rotgut
flag-waving cowardice. *Suffering Succotash*, sputters

Sylvester the Cat; *sine die*, say the pork-bellied legislators
of the swamps and plains. I miss all those guys, their Tweety-bird
       resilience, their Doris Day optimism, the candid unguent
of utter unhappiness on every channel, the midnight televangelist
       euphoric stew, the junk mail, voice mail vernacular.
On every *boulevard* and *rue* I miss the Tarzan cry of Johnny
       Weismueller, Johnny Cash, Johnny B. Goode,
and all the smart-talking, gum-snapping hard-girl dialogue,
       finger-popping x-rated street talk, sports babble,
Cheetoes, Cheerios, chili dog diatribes. Yeah, I miss them all,
       sitting here on my sidewalk throne sipping champagne
verses lined up like hearses, metaphors juking, nouns zipping
       in my head like Corvettes on Dexedrine, French verbs
slitting my throat, yearning for James Dean to jump my curb.

Brain Radio Harangue

I'm never more American than in another country,
  Jerry Lee Lewis chasing me down the Champs-Elysées,
the Big Bopper singing "Chantilly Lace" as I eat my *gateau*
  au chocolat avec chantilly, Roy Orbison "Crying"
when I feel homesick in the middle of November, wanting
  barbecue potato chips more than any dada pastry,
hearing Miles Davis in some restaurant, his horn like a disease
  in my blood or Elvis like an affliction in my hips,
flinging me down in the Luxembourg gardens, fucking me
  senseless or buying me a Cadillac convertible.
Which would be better or worse? Let's get our guitars
  straight on this, *Good golly, Miss Molly*, what am I doing
here, out of my element but dressed for the occasion,
  à la chinoise, lacquered sticks holding my hair
in some kind of confusion, like the city, flower shops
  with great tubs of calla lilies, a woman with her hand out,
"Madame, madame," snow rippling through the night like white
  flowers, and Jimi Hendrix singing, *There must be some way
out of here,* and there is, accidentally or on purpose,
  s'il vous plaît, Sylvia Plath or Tsvetsaeva, stalking her
tortured path through the Marais. Choose this corner
  left or right and everything could be completely changed.
Where's my lucky turn, my catastrophic corner, my meeting
  with Modigliani or the gestapo? I drag my wounded leg
up a stairway in the palace of unanswered questions, most
  of which can be translated, *Qui êtes vous?* I'm nobody,
who are you? Oh, Auntie Em, what's a girl to do, stuck inside
  of Paris with the Deep South blues again? Dreaming
of August, 100 percent humidity, and the slow drawl of endless
  afternoons, sliding on down to the coast
for a couple dozen oysters, but it's winter and we stroll down

the rue St. Jacques for *les huîtres*, green-skirted *marennes*
and a bottle of Muscadet. Oh, yes, I am under the influence
of something delirious here on the Pont Marie,
the pointed bustle of the Ile de la Cité dragging the river.
Where are you? calls my sister in an eternal game
of hide and seek, *What do you want?* exclaims a parade
of ex-friends, to which you reply, *Here I am,*
Nothing, Return to Sender, because I am nowhere finally,
a transient connection in the Milky Way, standing
under a street light, understanding nothing, I am no one, at last.

The Tawdry Masks of Women

Every bus ride is theater, giddy schoolgirls trying on
the tawdry masks of women, flirting with my nephew,

red and green lights, shop windows piled high, gold
glistered skeletal mannequins in slips of iridescent silk.

At night in the wind blowing over the Pont Marie I hear
Camille Claudel crying from the walls of her studio,

and two days before Christmas Elliot and I stand
miraculously alone before *La Gioconde,* follow her eyes,

cracked surface of her skin like softest sand before the deep
water of her mouth, and later standing in the cold

our Buddhist *gardienne* Nadine tells me in rapid-fire French
that in all things she tries to remain neutral, *neutre, neutre,*

neutre, the only word finally I understand in the barrage
tumbling out of her mouth like a waterfall, but I can't be

neutral, passion welling up in my heart for the exhausted maids,
dapper men in berets, the madwoman on the PC bus,

screaming, *Salope, salope,* as she descends at the Pont d'Ivry,
and everyone on the bus looking at each other, *Whore?*

Who's the whore here? or the chic older woman, leather pants
baggy on her skinny shanks, reading a battered paperback

Rimbaud as we take the bus to see Pasolini's *Canterbury Tales*,
the master himself as Chaucer, spinning his ribald stories

of human folly, each one a mirror, and when I see myself
in bus windows or store glass, the shock never wears off,

for I recognize myself and see a stranger at the same time,
because the minutes are racing by at the speed of light,

and I am saying goodbye to Paris, to everyone, myself
most of all, watching her disappear down the rue Jeanne d'Arc,

and what can she possibly be thinking as she walks
to the movies in the middle of this afternoon of her life?

III

American Odes

It occurs to me I am America.
I'm talking to myself again.
ALLEN GINSBERG

Ode to Hardware Stores

Where have all the hardware stores gone——dusty, sixty-watt
    warrens with wood floors, cracked linoleum,
poured concrete painted blood red? Where are Eppes, Terry Rosa,
    Yon's, Flint——low buildings on South Monroe,
Eighth Avenue, Gaines Street with their scent of paint thinner,
    pesticides, plastic hoses coiled like serpents
in a garden paradisal with screws in buckets or bins
    against a brick wall with hand-lettered signs
in ball-point pen——*Carriage screws, two dozen for fifty cents*——
    long vicious dry-wall screws, thick wood screws
like peasants digging potatoes in fields, thin elegant trim
    screws——New York dames at a backwoods hick
Sunday School picnic. O universal clevis pins, seven holes
    in the shank, like the seven deadly sins.
Where are the men——Mr. Franks, Mr. Piggot, Tyrone, Hank,
    Ralph——sunburnt with stomachs and no asses,
men who knew the mythology of nails, Zeuses enthroned
    on an Olympus of weak coffee, bad haircuts,
and tin cans of galvanized casing nails, sinker nails, brads,
    20-penny common nails, duplex head nails, flooring nails
like railroad spikes, finish nails, fence staples, cotter pins,
    roofing nails——flat-headed as Floyd Crawford,
who lived next door to you for years but would never say hi
    or make eye contact. What a career in hardware
he could have had, his blue-black hair slicked back with brilliantine,
    rolling a toothpick between his teeth while sorting
screw eyes and carpet tacks. Where are the hardware stores,
    open Monday through Friday, Saturday till two?
No night hours here, like physicists their universe mathematical
    and pure in its way: dinner at six, *Rawhide* at eight,
lights out at ten, kiss in the dark, up at five for the subatomic world

of toggle bolts, cap screws, hinch-pin clips, split-lock
washers. And the tools—saws, rakes, wrenches, rachets, drills,
        chisels, and hose heads, hose couplings, sandpaper
(garnet, production, wet or dry), hinges, wire nails, caulk, nuts,
        lag screws, pulleys, vise grips, hexbolts, fender washers,
all in a primordial stew of laconic talk about football, baseball,
        who'll start for the Dodgers, St. Louis, the Phillies,
the Cubs? Walk around the block today and see their ghosts:
        abandoned lots, graffitti'd windows, and tacked
to backroom walls, pin-up calendars almost decorous
        in our porn-riddled galaxy of Walmarts, Seven-Elevens,
stripmalls like strip mines or a carrion bird's curved beak
        gobbling farms, meadows, wildflowers, drowsy afternoons
of nothing to do but watch dust motes dance through a streak
        of sunlight in a darkened room. If there's a second coming,
I want angels called Lem, Nelson, Rodney, and Cletis gathered
        around a bin of nails, their silence like hosannahs,
hallelujahs, amens swelling from cinderblock cathedrals
        drowning our cries of *Bigger, faster, more, more, more.*

Ode to Barbecue

We are lost again in the middle of redneck nowhere,
    which is a hundred times scarier
than any other nowhere because everyone has guns.
    Let me emphasize that plural—rifles,
double-barreled shotguns, .22 semiautomatics,
    12-gauge pumps, .357 magnums. And for what?
Barbecue. A friend of a friend's student's cousin's
    aunt's husband was a cook in the army
for 30 years, and he has retired to rural Georgia
    with the sole aim in his artistic soul of creating
the best barbecued ribs in the universe and, according
    to rumor, he has succeeded, which is not surprising
because this is a part of the world where the artistic soul
    rises up like a phoenix from the pit of rattlesnake
churches and born-again retribution, where Charlie Lucas
    the Tin Man creates dinosaurs, colossi of rusted
steel bands and garbage can mamas with radiator torsos,
    electric-coil hearts, screw fingers. Here W.C. Rice's
Cross Garden grows out of the southern red clay with rusted
    Buicks shouting, "The Devil Will Put Your Soul
in Hell Burn it Forever" and "No Water in Hell," and I think
    of Chet Baker singing "Let's Get Lost," and I know
what he means, because more and more I know
    where I am, and I don't like the feeling,
and Chet knew about Hell and maybe about being saved,
    something much talked about in the Deep South,
being saved and being lost because we are all sinners,
    amen, we bear Adam's stain, and the only way
to heaven is to be washed in the blood of the Lamb,
    which is kind of what happens when out of the South
Georgia woods we see a little shack with smoke

pouring from the chimney though it's August
and steamier than a mild day in Hell; we sit at a picnic table
    and a broad-bellied man sets down plates of ribs,
a small mountain of red meat, so different from Paris
    where for my birthday my husband took me
to an elegant place where we ate tiny ribs washed down
    with a sublime St.-Josèphe. Oh, don't get me wrong,
they were good, but the whole time I was out of sorts,
    squirming on my perfect chair, disgruntled,
because I wanted to be at Tiny Register's, Kojack's,
    J.B.'s, I wanted ribs all right but big juicy ribs dripping
with sauce, the secret recipe handed down from grandmother
    to father to son, sauce that could take the paint off a Buick,
a hot, sin-lacerating concoction of tomatoes, jalapeños,
    and sugar, washed down with iced tea, Coca-Cola, beer,
because there's no water in Hell, and Hell is hot, oh yeah.

Ode on Satan's Power

At a local bistro's Christmas sing-along, the new
    age pianist leads us in a pan-cultural brew
of seasonal songs, the Ramadan chant being my
    personal favorite, though the Kwanza lullaby
and Hanukkah round are *very interesting*. Let's
    face it, most of us are there for the carols we set
to memory in childhood though some lyrics have been
    changed, so when we sing "God Rest Ye Merry, Gentlemen,"
we're transformed into a roomful of slightly tipsy
    middle-class *gentlepeople* who are longing to be
saved from *hopelessness* instead of *Satan's power when*
    we were gone astray, but I, for one, sing out *Satan's*
power as do most of the *gentlepeople*, women

and men, something I find myself pondering a few
    days later, while my profoundly worried nephew,
Henry, and I embark on our annual blitzkrieg
    of baking, punctuated by Henry's high speed
philosophical questioning, such as, Where do we
    go when we die? Pressing my collection of cookie
cutters—trees, snowflakes, Santas—into fragrant ginger
    dough, I want to say, *Who cares? Carpe diem, buster*,
though, of course, I'm way too scarred by pop psychology
    to utter half the nutty things that pop up like weeds
in the 18th-century garden of my brain. Eight-
    year-olds need their questions answered, I suppose, but not
by me. "Let's watch some TV," I say, an instrument

of Satan if ever there was one. *Bullitt's* on—Steve
    McQueen in his prime. I love this movie—equal waves
of sorrow and carnage washed up on a hokey late-

sixties beach of masculine cool. McQueen is Bullitt,
and Jacqueline Bisset's his girl. Henry and I start
    watching during the scene where she is driving Bullitt
around because, if I remember correctly, he's
    totaled not just one but several cars in at least
as many now-famous chases. Jackie drops Bullitt
    at a hotel, where he finds a girl, newly dead, throat
circled with purple fingerprints like grape jam stains. "What
    happened to her?" Henry asks, frowning. I think, *Oh, shit,*
this is not an officially approved nephew-aunt

Christmas activity. If I don't make a big deal
    of it, maybe he won't tell his mother. "Someone strangled
her," I say. "What's strangled?" he asks, and I see my sister
    has chosen not to threaten her child as our own dear
mother routinely threatened us. Driven crazy, she
    browbeat us with strangulation, being slapped silly,
public humiliation, murder, and eternal
    damnation. Perhaps because Henry's her only child,
my sister can afford to be gentler with her son,
    or maybe it's because two months before he was born
she almost lost him, ending up in the hospital,
    hooked to machines, ordered to bed for the final
wrenching weeks. Maybe that's why the story of the Christ child

speaks to us. All parents wonder how the world will treat
    their tender babes. Like Lorca, will he become a great
poet, then end up in a mass grave? Only German
    philosophers think more about death than Henry Gwynn.
"Why did he strangle her?" he asks, face formidable
    as Hegel's. *Satan's power*, I want to scream, but mumble
"It's just a movie; it's not real." Steve McQueen's dodging
    a plane, and I remember reading he did his own
stunts, which I tell Henry, but he's still in that hotel
    room. "If she was alive, how'd she get her eyes to roll

back into her head?" I'm thinking of pornography,
    snuff movies, all the things I never want him to see
or even know about in this tawdry world. "Honey,

it's a major motion picture. Even in a small part
    an actress has to be great." He nods and takes a bite
off Santa's head. "She was a pretty good actress." You
    bet your booty, and I realize out of the blue
Santa is an anagram for Satan. No way am
    I going to explain anagrams or Herr Satan,
though how wonderful to have such a nemesis—
    a fallen archangel, one of high heaven's brightest stars—
in a battle with Jehovah for our souls, rather
    than the calendar's increasing speed like a roller
coaster run amok through a fun park of lost dreams, lost
    landscapes, and children, growing up faster than we thought
possible in the last terrible days before their birth.

Ode on My Waist

Negative numbers were a mystery till the summer
    I turned fifteen and acquired a waist,
one day a human hotdog the next Brigitte Bardot,
    well, not her but in the same category,
And God Created Woman, not from Adam's rib
    but from a little girl, one day playing Barbies,
the next day initiated into the swirling world
    of algebraic reverses, rib cage on the hypotenuse
of the hip, gauge the indent, a new paragraph
    in the book of lust, boys sniffing like a pack
of hounds, the mathematics of breeding wrapped
    in the high-gloss patina of mini skirts and push-up
bras, magazines telling me how to walk, sit, smile,
    cross my legs, cross my heart, act stupid,
act smart, not knowing the dark chasm I was stepping
    into, the fissure of Scarlett's 18 inches,
the history of waists, Peloponnesian isthmus—corseted
    Athenian bosom at war with girdled Spartan hips—
how to end up without a swollen waist, captive slave
    in the marketplace of K through 12? O Solomon,
how could you forget the waist in your immortal song?
    Thy navel is like a round goblet, thy belly
like a heap of wheat set about with lilies, thy waist a bay
    on the body's shore, the legs' tropical blossom,
equator of a world so mysterious we could almost
    circumnavigate it with our hands, then—poof—it flies
away like a flock of blackbirds in the white curve of the sky.

Ode on My Sharp Tongue

Being a cocktail waitress did nothing for my eternal,
        most high and holy inviolate numinous soul,
because it took me almost no time to figure out
        that by being mean I raked in more loot,
my only aim in working in these smoky dens
        of iniquity, and as a vegetarian
and nondrinker, you can imagine how much better
        I thought I was than the office workers
and politicians who swilled gin deep into the night.
        These men liked my sharp tongue, my absolute
boredom with their admiration. Like Beatrice
        in *Much Ado* I was Lady Disdain but with twice
the venom because my mind was filled with Keats, Donne,
        their Truth and Beauty, sonnets, holy and un-

while I spent nights serving martinis and Manhattans,
        to a crowd of orangutans in the guise of men
and women, too, though they were rarely a problem. They'd
        down their drinks quietly, faces sliding to one side,
smiles gooey with something other than lust
        as they talked to these utter baboons who must
have had something to offer, if only sperm and a paycheck,
        in the biological roundelay. But the thick necks
and clumsy hands, more like the paws of some forest
        creature than a man—how could they bear it?
"Wake up," my mother used to say, "you're living
        in a dream world." Oh, Mom, I was waking
to a world where Beauty meant nothing, my heart hard
        as if I were eating bacon and eggs fried in lard

each morning before going off to class to talk
        about Yeats and Maude Gonne and then walking

to the Mecca to drink coffee that was bitter and weak
       at the same time. How unspeakably
beautiful my life was then, though how was I
       to know, being young and insufferably high-
minded, most nights going out into the parking lot, to yell
       into the black sky, "blow your trumpets, angels,
and arise, arise from death," as if anyone, even Donne,
       could change the world with something so one-
dimensional as faith. I had none, and nothing
       to take its place but poetry, my shining
girl, too radiant for any mortal man, though some tried,
       even the goons I served drinks to on Saturday night.

I had a pop quiz for men who wanted to date me, one
       no one could pass; some would even
ask to take it home, and I'd say, Sure, knowing
       each hungover one would wake the next morning
and think, "I'm a lawyer, and I'm taking a quiz
       written by a cocktail waitress?" Then his
ego would assume its natural splendor and go consume
       its day, and I was left feeling like some
character in a novel by Dostoyevsky, mostly Prince Myshkin,
       though sometimes Raskolnikov or even
Alyosha Karamazov. Beelzebub had left Moscow
       with Uncle Joe and come to our little cow
town, his acolytes walking the streets, appearing in
       public places, the cat, the redhead, these men,

like the law professor coming in with his wife, then
       returning alone to ask me out, the shmendrick.
Towering over him, I said I would if he'd bring a note from
       his wife, and he did. So this is what I'd come
to in my search for Truth and Beauty. I understood
       Keats's last days in Rome, his heart wooden
with bitterness, feeling as if his name were "writ

in water." Where is that girl today? It wouldn't
surprise me to pass her on the street, braless,
        in bell bottoms, a stack of Russian novels
in her arms, furious at Tolstoy for killing Prince Andrei,
        thinking she is some kind of modern day
Elizabeth Bennet, sneering at the older woman she's
        become. But she doesn't see me in her daze

of books and words. Oh, I'd love to kiss her face,
        my glimmering girl. How stupid she is, graceful
and young. Would she believe that one day she might
        feel for Mr. Casaubon or Mrs. Bennet
or even Mr. Collins, those villainous or comic
        characters, who never play the romantic
leads but toil at unfinished books, fall in love where
        no love waits for them. She'd laugh, I'm sure,
and I want it no other way, for sometimes late
        at night, bitterness will clutch my heart,
and that unhappy girl rises up from my throat,
        enamored of Keats, Rimbaud, his drunken boat,
shouting poems at the sky, drunk on words,
        in a sea of men drinking what she serves.

Ode to W. E. Diemer, the Inventor of Bubblegum

"It was an accident," he said and pink because red food
        coloring was all he had, much as the dictionary
of invention begins with agriculture and ends with wigs,
        and who knew the Chinese were so johnny-
on-the-spot, though explosives and chemical fertilizers
        have caused us no end of trouble, but color printing,
who has that hurt? Though moveable type has landed
        thousands in the hoosegow, and 400 years
before Gutenberg, Pi Cheng was setting his clay characters
        in an iron frame. Not to mention banknotes, chess,
square roots, gun powder, and iron—all born in China,

while the Mesopotamians were figuring out agriculture
        and insurance, and in the scheme of things
wheat and barley have to go to the head of the line
        as far as forwarding the human endeavor,
while bubblegum, alas, to the tail end, because if man
        cannot live by bread alone, we certainly
can't get by on a diet of bubblegum, though pink
        is sublime, a color invented by Hieronymus Bosch
in 1510, because until his *Garden of Earthly Delights*
        pink did not exist in its present form. Oh,
there was a Perugino rose, a Botticelli pale cherry,

a Leonardo blush, but before Bosch's otherworldly
        carapaces, giant birds, cherries, plums, apples
was there pink? I think not. Until Bosch, Christ
        was robed in blue with a gold-leaf nimbus,
and a bunch of sad-sack disciples hanging around, no
        surprises there—betrayal, crucifixion, Golgotha—
but Bosch's Christ is in pink, his men and women embracing

giant strawberries, standing on their heads
and kissing, consorting with mermaids, catching a ride
on a flying fish, gazing at their plum-headed
darlings. Is there anything so tender as the duck proffering

a cherry while nestled on the bent knees of a man
doing a handstand encased in an egg?
Even in Hell pinks reign supreme—a menacing bagpipe,
Satan's robe, the flesh of a portly froglike creature
reading music written on a woman's buttocks.
And where would the last half of the twentieth century
be without bubblegum—the thing, the color, the word?
The radio was awash with it until that fateful
New-Year's-day countdown of 1968 when The Weird
Beard announced on K-POI in Honolulu
that the Rolling Stones had usurped The Association's

stranglehold on number one, because you can't get no,
no, no, no. We'd been psychedelicized,
and bubblegum pink became hot pink, acid pink,
diabolic pink, and for a moment we'd landed
again in *The Garden of Earthly Delights*, though aerial
copulation with mermaids soon dissolved
into frigid ice-skating through the hell of the seventies,
disco and stacked heels, tight jeans and mullets.
Cut off my ear, Vincent, and throw it on the devil's pyre
at the end of the driveway, for I am Mesopotamian
at heart, my garden a riot of tomatoes, strawberries, heavenly

pinks of plumeria and stock, watermelon and ginger,
simmering in the sun. Oh, let us praise all acts
of conception—Julius Caesar for inventing the newspaper;
Archimedes for the screw; Hero of Alexandria
for his steam engine; Fang Feng for the universal joint;
Gabriele Fallopio for seeing pigs' intestines

and thinking "condoms," and the Egyptians, for the pen,
    clock, saw, glue, arch, file, mirror, and the wig,
of course, which covers the skull, carapace of the brain,
    dream-center of the universe, inventor of heaven
and hell, our soft pink big-bang bubblegum of unearthly delight.

Ode to Rock 'n' Roll

Tonight the band is so good you have to dance, the lead
    singer's voice like honey at the bottom of a jar,
so deep your hand gets stuck, fingers skimming the last
    bead of sweet, so sticky you remember riding
in a car, an MG or midnight blue Mustang,
    through a fragrant tropical night, 1969 it was,
the radio playing "Ain't Too Proud to Beg,"
    only you were, didn't even know what begging was,
but now you know. Oh, you've done some begging
    in your time, been way down, so low you thought
you'd never get up, because you'd been that bad; you'd lied,
    cheated, stolen, or that's what the falsetto
is singing, swooping down like a crazy mockingbird
    after an alley cat, scratching your skin,
making your tired bones loose in their sockets, and you're
    shaking it, moving your hips like you was some kind
of home girl, jumping up like that skinny cat on a hot
    sidewalk. You're frying eggs, mama, the bald drummer
telling you how to cut that particular rug into a thousand pieces,
    your feet religious, your knees like holy water,
head crazy with hair, the wild Indian your mother
    always said you were, but a Comanche, whose word
for themselves means *the human beings* and that's what you are,
    finally, in this sweltering room in the middle
of December, your arms moving like a semaphore,
    as if you were frantically trying to signal
a distant ship in the doom of the night, an ark filled
    with such fear the Bantu word *mbuki-mvuki*,
to tear off your clothes to dance, is almost lost till it floats
    back on the Mississippi as *boogie-woogie*
in a wild trance of forgetting, and sometimes the spot

on your sullen heart is the sweetest part,
this collision of Bantu, blues, hillbilly riffs, riding the night
        like a wild stallion filled with a murderous longing.
Oh, let there be fire, a sulfurous kindling of earth and air,
        and in the clear morning may we all be Comanches,
riding the high plains of indifferent grass, fierce with the murmur
        of gods—Leadbelly's growl, Hendrix's response,
Little Richard's screams, heaven sent as our own voices
        were we human enough to heed the call.

Ode to My 1977 Toyota

Engine like a Singer sewing machine, where have you
    not carried me—to dance class, grocery shopping,
into the heart of darkness and back again? O the fruit
    you've transported—cherries, peaches, blueberries,
watermelons, thousands of Fuji apples—books,
    and all my dark thoughts, the giddy ones, too,
like bottles of champagne popped at the wedding of two people
    who will pass each other on the street as strangers
in twenty years. Ronald Reagan was president when I walked
    into Big Chief Motors and saw you glimmering
on the lot like a slice of broiled mahi mahi or sushi
    without its topknot of tuna. Remember the months
I drove you to work singing "Some Enchanted Evening"?
    Those were scary times. All I thought about
was getting on I-10 with you and not stopping. Would you
    have made it to New Orleans? What would our life
have been like there? I'd forgotten about poetry. Thank God,
    I remembered her. She saved us both. We were young
together. Now we're not. College boys stop us at traffic lights
    and tell me how cool you are. Like an ice cube, I say,
though you've never had air conditioning. Who needed it?
    I would have missed so many smells without you—
confederate jasmine, magnolia blossoms, the briny sigh
    of the Gulf of Mexico, rotting 'possums scattered
along 319 between Sopchoppy and Panacea. How many holes
    are there in the ballet shoes in your back seat?
How did that pair of men's white loafers end up in your trunk?
    Why do I have so many questions, and why
are the answers like the animals that dart in front of your headlights
    as we drive home from the coast, the Milky Way
strung across the black velvet bowl of the sky like the tiara
    of some impossibly fat empress who rules the universe
but doesn't know if tomorrow is December or Tuesday or June first.

Ode on My Mother's Handwriting

Her *a*'s are like small rolls warm from the oven, yeasty,
    fragrant, one identical to the other, molded
by a master baker, serious about her craft, but comical, too,
    smudge of flour on her sharp nose, laughing
with her workers, urging them to eat, eat, eat, but demanding
    the most gorgeous cakes in Christendom.
Her *b*'s are upright as soldiers trained by harsh sergeants,
    whose invective seems cruel in the bower of one's
own country but becomes hot gruel and a wool coat
    during January on the steppes outside Moscow.
Would that every infant could nestle in the warm crook
    of her *c*'s, taste the sweet milk of her *d*'s, hear
the satiny coos of her nonsense whisperings, making
    the three-pronged razor of her *E* easier to take,
the *bad girl, I'm ashamed of you, disappointed, hateful,*
    shame, shame, shame, the blistering fury
of her *f* feel less like the sharpened rapier of a paid assassin,
    left only with the desire to be good, to be ushered
again into the glittering palace of her good graces,
    for her *g*'s are great and fail not, their mercy
is everlasting. The house of her *h* is a plain building. It has no
    pediments or Palladian windows but brick walls,
sturdy and indestructible. Oh, the mighty storms that rage
    cannot tear down these thick walls or alter
their sturdy heart. But her windows are small—she does not
    like to look out, shuts her eyes, for the world
is cold while her fire is warm. She is a household god,
    jumped up on Jesus, Jeremiah, Job, all the Old
Testament scallywags and their raving pomaded televangelist
    progeny, yet her *k*'s know how to kick up their heels,
laugh at you and with you, whip up a Christmas Dickens

would envy, kiss your eyelids as you drift off to sleep,
though no one can know the loneliness of her *l*, a forlorn
    obelisk in the desert, hard and bitterly cold
in the heat of the sun. Other *m*'s are soft and round,
    but not hers—the answer to every supplication
is, "N-O spells no," which, in a way, is comforting,
    because you know where you stand,
where your please, *pretty please* begins, and how far those *p*'s
    must climb before meeting her most serene
and imperial *q*'s—regular, rigid, redoubtable. For the dark wind
    of her *s*'s can be like the desert simoom, hot and dry.
You could die of thirst, your throat taut as a tent pole holding up
    your bones and their tatters of flesh, but for her hurricane
of words, blowing roofs off houses, lavishing water on an arid world,
    unleashing slaps, hugs, prayers on the long, ungainly hours
that separate us like the spaces between her lines, the waves
    of her *u*'s, slice of her *v*'s, vivisecting each moment
with the x-ray of her ecclesiastical gaze. What is her *x*, a kiss
    or a rebuke? Both—her lips sweet as the nectar
bees suck from flowers, cruel as their sting. So why
    am I still her acolyte, her disciple, her most obstreperous
slave? Because in the curve of her *zed* is my Zen master,
    my beginning and my end. How I have felt the five
fingers of her one hand; seen her hair, once chestnut, turn white
    as a seraph's wings; heard her high, naked voice combust
with love's bitter perfume; sat down at her Puritan
    table and feasted on her wild blue eyes, like rustling
cornflowers in the dark, mutinous grass of the past.

Ode to the Bride of Frankenstein

I'm in a dim Chinese restaurant in Hollywood
    with my boyfriend, Mr. Wait-a-Minute, Mr. Should-
have-Could-have-Would-have, the Marquis of Maybe-Baby,
    Prince of the Past Tense, last Emperor of Whoa-Nelly,
and I am not talking love and marriage, though that too,
    but whether to order Szechuan Beef or Mu Shu
Pork, and since I took exactly two minutes to choose
    Shrimp with Lobster Sauce, while my dear companion loses
his marbles over the crimson-backed menu I am
    free to survey the dark, lantern-festooned oblong room,
which is not crowded because it's only six-thirty,
    and after taking in the whole dismal menagerie,
my eyes settle on an older woman with blowzy

grey hair, wearing a muumuu, peering through bifocals
    at a man, too handsome to be heterosexual,
maybe thirty, and he's listening to her as she waves
    her hand in circles like a doomed helicopter, saved
from a last minute crash landing on the table. There's
    such a wrinkle between the young man's brows, I would swear
something is at stake, maybe money—she's his childless
    great-aunt Claudia, and why shouldn't he have the best
part of her gazillions instead of his stuck-up bitch
    of a sister, who will either end up in a ditch,
knife in her back, or ruling the world. I'm all for him
    since he probably chose between the Hot Kung Pow Shrimp
and Spicy General Tso Chicken in under ten

minutes, so the oldest woman in this cheap Chinese
    bordello has a better date than I do, which, please
God, is true, of every last woman in the greater

Los Angeles area, except the wives of your
ax murders and pedophiles who happen to be
        out of the joint between crimes, though even they can be
tender at home, I've read, saving their blood lust for work.
        Though I know it's utterly pointless, I sneak a look
at my boyfriend, who's running his finger down the page
        of tofu fried rice dishes, and in a pop of rage
I recognize the older woman—she is the Bride
        of Frankenstein, the great Elsa Lanchester, who I'd
have sworn on a stack of Bibles probably had died

years ago, but there she sits with her decisive young
        man, eating a tasty Kon Pow Chicken or Peking
Duck and talking about whatever the most-famous-
        female-horror-star-ever talks about over rice
and Shanghai Beef. When the movie opens she's Mary
        Shelley in a stadium-lit 18th-century
drawing room, laughing madly with Percy and Byron,
        but she quickly becomes the tortured bride of her own
wayward imagination, a woman created
        by Dr. Frankenstein for his lonely blockheaded
monster. But this time the doctor cooks up a stunning
        creature, a belle with a weird 'do, upswept with lightning
bolt white streaks jetting out from her temples. Rejecting

her hideous beau, the bride is abducted by him,
        and I can't remember the rest, though like other dim
bulb, snippy beauties in film, I'm sure it's not champagne
        and kisses but more like *House of Wax*'s steady rain,
through which Vincent Price scurries to kidnap loose shopgirls,
        then kill and cover them with hot paraffin and call
them Cleopatra and Florence Nightingale in his
        sinister Madame Tussaud's. Oh, there's Bela, Boris,
Lon Chaney, Peter Lorre—was he ever scary
        in *M*, skulking down alleys looking for unwary

girls to kill. Horror shows are full of funny uncles—
          evil, elegant men—John Carradine, the spectral
Christopher Lee, Peter Cushing, their impeccable

avuncular sneers, always ready with the coin, gum
          drop, or gold watch to hypnotize the big-eyed rube farm
girls with creamy skin, only in this, the final dregs
          of the century, any girl of a certain age,
farm bred or not, has seen, at least once, *I Drink Your Blood*,
          in which a group of nasty hippies quaffs the tired
plasma of a rabid dog, then turns into a gang
          of marauding cannibals, criminals, evil winged
monkeys searching Oz for good little girls, their dogs, tin
          men, scarecrows, quaking lions. I've wasted so much time
at the movies—you name it, I love them, musicals,
          whodunits, caper flicks, kung-fu films, historical
tearjerkers, Bing-and-Bob road fluff, anything by Buñuel,

and horror shows. I need to be scared out of my skin
          every minute of my life, especially the times when
I think I know what I'm doing or who I am. That's
          when *Carnival of Blood, Cauldron of Blood,* and *I Spit
on Your Grave* come in handy. Little Miss Know-It-All,
          I go into *Chopper Chicks in Zombietown* enthralled
with my own numinous personality, but leave
          a graduate of *Satan's School for Girls,* my right sleeve
dripping blood, neck sore from 360-degree
          rotations, or I decide to go to the movies
on Tuesday the fifth, but when I walk out it's *Friday
          the 13th, Part 4:The Final Chapter.* My dismay
is the only surprise, because it's the price we pay

for being alive—the *Terrorgram, Terrorvision,*
          squaring off against *Revenge of the Teenage Vixens
from Outer Space, Mutant on the Bounty,* and *Mothra,*

a Japanese movie, which chronicles the saga
of a pissed-off giant caterpillar who invades
 Tokyo, not to mention *The House That Dripped Blood,*
Horror Express, Horror Hotel, Horror Planet, Scream
 Blacula Scream, Spontaneous Combustion, but I'm
saved from the horror by a waiter who brings us Mai
 Tais with pink and yellow umbrellas, and every five-
year-old's dream food—maraschino cherries, which happen
 to be the very hue of the Bride of Frankenstein's
lips. Now we are ready to order eggrolls, won ton

soup and other yummy things, though while Elsa and her
 young man talk, I can't help but see the ghouls that hover
behind the plate glass window dividing our cozy
 haven from Sunset Boulevard. I feel like Mary
Shelley in her bright room with her tale of a woman
 brought back from the dead to a world of Moo Goo Gai Pan,
Buick sedans, and Vegematics—*A Comedy*
 of Terrors, but we each get the top billing, though we
are often forced to share the stage with men who can spend
 half an hour choosing the gross-out Ma Pa Bean Curd
and the dry husk, twice removed of the girl who gathered
 the dark bugs of the world into a story that sliced
the heart and dished it up with hot peppers and steamed rice.

Notes

"O Deceitful Tongue": Some of the odd and beautiful words in this poem were plundered from *Forgotten English: Vanishing Vocabulary and Folklore* by Jeffrey Kacirk.

"Fang": Fang is one of the four major Bantu tribes in the West African country of Gabon. Fang is also their language. I owe everything I know about this subject to a short article in a paper given to me by a British couple on a train from Naples to Rome in the summer of 2000. I don't remember the newspaper, but the article was entitled "192-part Guide to the World, Part 62: Gabon" by Jeremy Atiyah.

"Ode to Rock 'n' Roll": I am indebted to Howard Rheingold's book *They Have a Word for It* (Sarabande Books) for *mbuki-mvuki*.

"Ode to My 1977 Toyota": I couldn't have written this poem without Kenneth Koch's marvelous *New Addresses*. Thanks to Billy Collins for telling me about it.

Acknowledgments

Grateful acknowledgment is made to the journals in which these poems first appeared: *Boulevard* ("Ode to American English"); *Five Points* ("Calling the Friends of Friends," "Cinerama," "Left Bank Freudian Striptease," "Ode to Barbecue," and "Ode to the Bride of Frankenstein"); *Harvard Review* ("Shh"); *Indiana Review* ("Thus Spake the Mockingbird"); *Meridian* ("Ode on Satan's Power"); *Mississippi Review* ("Flesh, Bone, and Red" and "Ode on My Waist"); *Paris Review* ("Fang," "The Mockingbird on the Buddha," "Ode on My Mother's Handwriting," and "The Tawdry Masks of Women"); *Parnassus* ("Ode to Rock 'n' Roll"); *Ploughshares* ("My Translation"); *Poems and Plays* ("The History of Apples, Part I"); *POOL* ("Brain Radio Harangue"); *Runes* ("The Mockingbird Falls in Love" and "O Deceitful Tongue"); *Southern Poetry Review* ("Run"); *Southern Review* ("The Mockingbird Counts to Ten," "Ode to Hardware Stores," "Ode to My 1977 Toyota," "Six, Sex, Say," and "13th Arrondissement Blues"); *Triquarterly Review* ("Idolatry" and "The Mockingbird Invents Writing"); *Western Humanities Review* ("Attention, Citizen Sade," "Babel," and "Ode on My Sharp Tongue"); *Yale Review* ("Ode to W. E. Diemer, the Inventor of Bubblegum").

"Left Bank Freudian Striptease," "Cinerama," and "Ode to Barbecue" received the 2002 James Dickey Prize for Poetry given by *Five Points*.

The following poems were featured on *Poetry Daily*: "Six, Sex, Say" (April 18, 2001), "Idolatry" (May 22, 2002), "Left Bank Freudian Striptease" (December 26, 2002), and "Ode on Satan's Power" (February 23, 2003).

"Six, Sex, Say" also appeared in *Poetry Daily: 366 Poems from the World's Most Popular Poetry Website*, edited by Diane Boller, Don Selby, and Chryss Yost (Sourcebooks, 2003).

Without the everyday solace of my life with David Kirby, this book would not exist. He has read every poem and changed them all for the better. He's funny, smart, kind, and my truest friend.

I'd like to thank Steve Gehrke and Stephen Dunn for plucking my manuscript from oblivion, and I'd also like to express my deep gratitude to the magazine editors, who have been steadfast in their support, especially Michael Griffith of the *Southern Review*, David Bottoms and Megan Sexton of *Five Points*, Campbell McGrath in his peripatetic editorships at *Triquarterly* and *Ploughshares*, Herb Leibowitz of *Parnassus*, and Don Selby, Diane Boller, and Rob Anderson of *Poetry Daily*.

My most heartfelt thanks go to Richard Howard, who picked my work from the slush pile of the *Paris Review* and without whose longstanding encouragement I would certainly be a poorer person and a far more bedraggled poet. A poet, critic, and translator of immense accomplishment and capacious mind—he continually lends a hand to struggling writers as teacher, editor, and friend. Though I have never studied with him formally, he has taught me so much. He has praised and scolded me into being a better poet and through his example, I hope, a better teacher. It is with admiration, gratitude, and affection I dedicate this book to him.

Barbara Hamby is the author of *Delirium* (1995), which won the Vassar Miller Prize, the Poetry Society of America's Norma Farber First Book Award, and the Kate Tufts Award; and *The Alphabet of Desire* (1999), which won the 1998 New York University Poetry Prize and was chosen as one of the twenty-five best books of 1999 by the New York City Public Library. She and her husband, poet David Kirby, live in Tallahassee, Florida, where she teaches in the Creative Writing Program at Florida State University.